First Facts®

PREDATOR PROFILES

EAGLES

— BUILT FOR THE HUNT —

by Tammy Gagne

Consultant: Dr. Jackie Gai, DVM

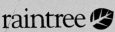

raintree
a Capstone company — publishers for children

Raintree is an imprint of Capstone Global Library Limited, a company incorporated in England and Wales having its registered office at 264 Banbury Road, Oxford, OX2 7DY – Registered company number: 6695582

www.raintree.co.uk
myorders@raintree.co.uk

Editorial Credits
Carrie Braulick Sheely, editor; Sarah Bennett and Juliette Peters, designers; Tracy Cummins, media researcher; Tori Abraham, production specialist

ISBN 9781474716840 (hardback)
20 19 18 17 16
10 9 8 7 6 5 4 3 2 1

ISBN 9781474716901 (paperback)
21 20 19 18 17
10 9 8 7 6 5 4 3 2 1

British Library Cataloguing in Publication Data
A full catalogue record for this book is available from the British Library.

Acknowledgements
We would like to thank the following for permission to reproduce photographs:
Getty Images: George Silk/Time & Life Pictures, 19, Guy Edwardes, 15; Shutterstock: Bildagentur Zoonar GmbH, 14, Capture Light, Cover, davemhuntphotography, 3, Donjiy, 12, FloridaStock, 5, Jean-Edouard Rozey, 21, martellostudio, 13, Nachiketa Bajaj, 6, Neil Burton, 8-9, ODM Studio, 16, Peter Krejzl, Cover Back, Peter Wey, 2, piotrwzk, 17, Sergey Uryadnikov, 10-11, Serjio74, 1, worldswildlifewonders, 7

Every effort has been made to contact copyright holders of material reproduced in this book. Any omissions will be rectified in subsequent printings if notice is given to the publisher.

All the internet addresses (URLs) given in this book were valid at the time of going to press. However, due to the dynamic nature of the internet, some addresses may have changed, or sites may have changed or ceased to exist since publication. While the author and publisher regret any inconvenience this may cause readers, no responsibility for any such changes can be accepted by either the author or the publisher.

Printed and bound in the United Kingdom.

CONTENTS

WASTING NO TIME

The lake water is barely moving. But the sharp-eyed eagle spots the salmon just below the water's surface. The hungry bird swoops down. Dipping only its feet into the water, the eagle grabs the fish with its long **talons**.

Eagles are among the world's most powerful **predators**. They are called birds of **prey** or raptors because they mainly hunt other animals for food.

FACT

More than 60 eagle **species** live throughout the world. Most are found in Africa, Asia and Europe. Only bald and golden eagles live in North America.

talon a long, sharp claw
predator an animal that hunts other animals for food
prey an animal hunted by another animal for food
species a group of animals with similar features

DON'T BE PICKY!

Eagles live where they can get food. Most eagles nest on cliffs or in the tops of tall trees. They can see prey better from up above. Many eagles live close to water where fish such as salmon, herring and catfish are plentiful. Eagles also eat smaller birds and land animals, such as rabbits. The harpy eagle is the largest eagle species. It eats monkeys and sloths. Some eagles will even feast on **carrion** left behind by other predators.

serpent eagle

FACT
The serpent eagle is named for the prey it hunts. This species eats **reptiles** such as snakes, frogs and lizards.

carrion dead, rotting flesh

reptile a cold-blooded animal that breathes air and has a backbone; most reptiles have scales

harpy eagle

CLEVER HUNTERS

Eagles hunt during the day. Most eagles hunt alone. But sometimes two bald eagles will pair up to make the job easier. One bird flies near the ground to **flush** small birds from trees and bushes. The other eagle perches nearby so it can snatch the prey from the air. Once the prey has been caught, the eagles share the meal.

FACT
Some eagles even walk along the ground and grab prey out of holes.

flush to cause to take flight suddenly

STEALING FOOD

Eagles sometimes steal fish from other birds. An eagle will chase and pester the other bird in midair. It won't stop until the other predator drops its kill. Often the eagle will then catch the prey in its talons while it is still falling.

FACT
Bald eagles have been known to steal fish from people's fishing rods.

AN EYE FOR THE HUNT

Eagles have excellent eyesight. They can see both in front of them and to each side at the same time. Just as important, eagles can see objects both near and far away. A golden eagle can spot a rabbit from up to 1.6 kilometres (1 mile) away.

FACT
An eagle's vision is at least four times sharper than a person's.

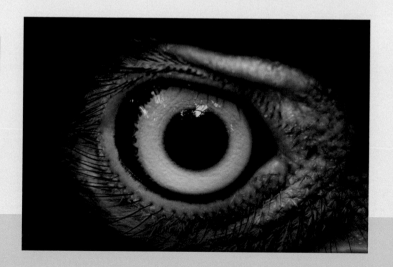

13

FAST IN FLIGHT

Eagles are fast fliers. Golden eagles are the fastest eagles. While flying level through the air, they can reach 129 km (80 mi) per hour. Once a golden eagle spots prey, it's time for the big dive! A golden eagle can dive at speeds of up to 322 km (200 mi) per hour.

FACT

Bald eagles can dive at speeds approaching 161 km (100 mi) per hour.

a golden eagle in flight

A golden eagle reaches for its prey.

MEAL TIME

Eagles kill prey with their sharp talons. These powerful claws rip through animal flesh like knives. Eagles also rely on their hooked beaks for tearing flesh off their kills. Since they have no teeth, eagles swallow these chunks of meat whole.

FACT

A **myth** says that once an eagle grabs prey with its talons, the eagle can't let go. This idea that the talons lock around the prey isn't true. But few prey animals can escape an eagle's powerful grip.

myth a false idea that many people believe

STRONG IN BODY AND MIND

The largest eagles can carry more than 4.5 kilogrammes (10 pounds). Some eagles put their strength to the test. A fish that weighs more than 2.3 kg (5 lb) is too heavy for a bald eagle to carry. Yet this eagle doesn't just give up. Many bald eagles will swim to shore with the prey instead of flying with it. They use their wings as paddles.

FACT

Some bald eagles are too stubborn for their own good. They drown trying to lift fish that are too heavy.

GROWING UP

Baby eagles are called eaglets. After **fledging**, the young birds learn to fly. While they practice flying, the parents bring food back to the nest. Eaglets learn to hunt by watching the adults. The young birds will grow up to be some of the most powerful predators in the world.

FACT
Eagles often use the same nest each year.

AMAZING BUT TRUE!
Bald eagles are known for building huge nests. It might take a pair of bald eagles at least two weeks to build their nest. The largest bald eagle nest ever found measured 3 metres (9.5 feet) wide and 6 m (20 ft) high. This incredible dwelling weighed more than 1.8 tonnes! That's equal to the weight of about four adult polar bears!

fledge to develop the feathers needed for flying

GLOSSARY

carrion dead, rotting flesh

fledge to develop the feathers needed for flying

flush to cause to take flight suddenly

level at the same height

myth a false idea that many people believe

predator an animal that hunts other animals for food

prey an animal hunted by another animal
for food

reptile a cold-blooded animal that breathes
air and has a backbone; most reptiles have scales

species a group of animals with similar features

talon a long, sharp claw, especially the claw of a bird
of prey

READ MORE

Bald Eagles (Animal Icons), Sheila Griffin Llanas (ABDO Pub., 2013).

Eagles (Seedlings), Kate Riggs (Creative Education, 2015).

The Eagles Are Back, Jean Craighead George (Dial Books for Young Readers, 2013).

WEBSITES

Animal Planet: Bald Eagle
http://www.animalplanet.com/wild-animals/bald-eagle/

BBC Nature: Tips for Identifying UK Birds of Prey
http://www.bbc.co.uk/nature/17826169

The RSPB: Golden Eagle
http://www.rspb.org.uk/discoverandenjoynature/
discoverandlearn/birdguide/name/g/goldeneagle/

COMPREHENSION QUESTIONS

1. Explain how the areas where eagles live help them find food.

2. Name three features that help eagles catch their prey. Which one of these do you think is most important? Why?

INDEX